SHE, BESIDE A FIRE

h.
SIN

SHE, BESIDE A FIRE

Your life has been a long story with chapters dedicated to heartache and the fight to start over. It's not like you want it that way. I think you set out to find someone you could live an entire lifetime beside but often times, you make the discovery that the person you chose just isn't up for choosing you.

You're left with all these questions and confusion. It's not right. You give your best and end up with nothing. You give your all and yet the other person lives in this delusional space where what you've given is someone not enough.

I want to say that I'm sorry that your experience in love has rendered you hurt and at times you've considered the impossibility of finding a love that matches the love in your heart but I don't want you to allow your past to dictate your future because nothing you left behind will ever compare to what's waiting for you. Something good is coming.

SHE, BESIDE A FIRE

I know you're struggling with finding a partner who is genuinely worthy of your devotion and energy. I know that it's been some time since you've known what an abundance of love and peace feels like during a relationship and there are times where you just want to give up but you have to remember that you are proof that real love exists because real love exists within you.

Understand that you are fully capable of being the love of your life while you preserve your heart for the love of your life. Something good is coming and I don't want you to allow your exes the power to make you stop believing in a love that will match your efforts and desire. I'm telling you this because I care about you and your heart!

SHE, BESIDE A FIRE

I know you don't want to leave them but please don't get lost there. Your heart is meant for so much more and maybe I just think that when you read these words, you'll take it as a sign and begin to let go.

When you settle for a love that feels small, you miss the chance to love someone who understands just how big your heart is.

SHE, BESIDE A FIRE

All the disappointments and dead ends have led you to this moment. The hurt, the sadness of it all, inspired you to look within, discovering your ability to heal your wounds using a magic that was kept hidden from you.

Look what you found inside yourself, a fountain for cleansing and a strength for withstanding things that were meant to break you down into impossible pieces.

I write this for you because I love what you're becoming. I write this for you because you're worth telling the world about. I write this for you because even on your toughest of days, you deserve to smile.

with love and respect, this is yours to keep...

SHE, BESIDE A FIRE

she's setting boundaries
she's being intentional
she's raising her frequency
she's processing
she's practicing acceptance
she's healing
she's not the woman
you tried to destroy
she's something different
someone you'll never be able
to comprehend or reach

SHE, BESIDE A FIRE

I had a dream about your awakening. It was the moment in which you realized that you were deserving of more than what you were given. You wanted to fight for someone who waged a war on your heart and so there was a moment where you decided to no longer run toward the things that caused you to compromise your peace and so the journey back to yourself began. I saw you fall and then rise. I watched you cut your finger tips on shards of your heart as you tried to piece yourself back together again and I know you're not fully healed. I know there are more steps to take on your journey but while you rest in this moment, while you pause to read my words. I just wanted to let you know that you are brilliantly beautiful wherever you are.

SHE, BESIDE A FIRE

A calm woman has clarity. The more clear she is about the way you've made her feel. The less likely she is to tolerate your shit.

SHE, BESIDE A FIRE

Self love helps you attract positive outcomes in relationships. Start with yourself when looking for someone to love.

SHE, BESIDE A FIRE

Alone and on your own is better than the loneliness you feel when you're clinging to the wrong person.

SHE, BESIDE A FIRE

The woman who masters watering herself isn't moved by empty gestures of interest. And it's going to take more than looks and pretty words to be granted a look into her heart.

SHE, BESIDE A FIRE

The woman who masters watering herself isn't moved by empty gestures of interest. And it's going to take more than looks and pretty words to be granted a look into her heart.

SHE, BESIDE A FIRE

I wonder where your heart moves when you think of love. I like to think that it turns inward first and after you've given yourself to yourself, I can only wish that you have something left for me.

You see, I'm okay with you choosing yourself first. I'm okay with this idea that you don't necessarily need anyone because you understand that you can be the source but still, I just hope that when you're ready to be loved. You allow me to do it.

SHE, BESIDE A FIRE

In the stillness of the chaos, she reclaimed power over her life. She reclaims a peace that was once kept from her.

SHE, BESIDE A FIRE

The love you deserve will not feel like a battleground, and the peace you seek exists in letting go.

SHE, BESIDE A FIRE

That's the thing. You thought you could confuse her heart and distract her from everything she deserved, but she changed the game once she remembered who she was.

SHE, BESIDE A FIRE

Beneath the scars that you've picked up along the way,
there lies a brilliant strength to live and love again.

SHE, BESIDE A FIRE

You offered her the world, but the universe was unfolding within her the entire time.

SHE, BESIDE A FIRE

The clarity and truth you are seeking exist in the depth of your tears. Within your pain, there is an answer.

SHE, BESIDE A FIRE

She's the type of woman who understands that beneath it all, her energy and light is meant for a beautiful relationship. She's the type of woman who understands that what she deserves is not too much to ask for. She's the type of a woman who understands her own power, she understands that she is the source of all things needed. This is why she's not moved by the bare minimum. This is why she chooses herself rather than settle for a relationship that can never bear fruit. This is why I'm writing this to her in hopes that she gets this message.

The thought of you is brilliant and rare. Never let them dim your light or make you forget just how wonderful you are.

SHE, BESIDE A FIRE

Walking away is not a loss. You gain so much more from life when you leave behind people who have been the biggest reasons behind your sadness.

SHE, BESIDE A FIRE

When it comes to love, I'd rather have nothing than half!

SHE, BESIDE A FIRE

Her heart heals, her mind clears, and life goes on to become more beautiful.

SHE, BESIDE A FIRE

Someday, when you've nearly given up on love, someone will waltz into your life to answer the question as to why it never worked out with another one else.

SHE, BESIDE A FIRE

I hope you find someone who understands the meaning of your silence. Someone who both appreciates the storm and your calm.

SHE, BESIDE A FIRE

Your soulmate will not always meet you at your best, but while you heal, they will appreciate the song even if the melody is a mess.

SHE, BESIDE A FIRE

What she craved was for someone to touch her soul long before they would touch her skin. She wanted to be moved by the stillness and confidence of someone who was certain about what they felt for her.

SHE, BESIDE A FIRE

She was a storm, the type you couldn't take your eyes off. The type of storm you couldn't believe until you saw it. The kind of storm someone runs towards without regret.

SHE, BESIDE A FIRE

SHE, BESIDE A FIRE

It's intriguing to believe that the most familiar sense of home will come in the form of the glance and voice of a stranger. And even with the unknowns, you'll know that they are the one.

SHE, BESIDE A FIRE

Within the silent chambers of her soul, she waged a silent battle for the love she deserved.

SHE, BESIDE A FIRE

She's the only ocean that inspired me to swim.

SHE, BESIDE A FIRE

Understand this...

Letting go simply means that you've arrived at the realization that some people can only be recorded as part of your history, as they do not deserve to exist in the realm of your destiny.

SHE, BESIDE A FIRE

She built a fortress around her heart and challenged anyone who wanted her love to prove that they were deserving.

SHE, BESIDE A FIRE

She discovered that she herself was on a never-ending journey with the ability to change directions if where she was headed turned out to be a destination that didn't align with her future self.

SHE, BESIDE A FIRE

What she discovered once she began to look inward was the ability and power to heal, to love completely, and to start anew.

SHE, BESIDE A FIRE

she sat in the middle of the chaos
and cultivated the most beautiful calm

SHE, BESIDE A FIRE

Love her fiercely, for her heart is a wild thing, and in that wildness lies her true beauty.

SHE, BESIDE A FIRE

Within every ending, there is a whisper of hope that gives life to a new beginning. In every goodbye, the hope of the most beautiful hello.

SHE, BESIDE A FIRE

I leveled up when you left.
I leveled up in your absence.
I leveled up when it ended.
I leveled up by letting go.
I leveled up when you left.
I leveled up in your absence.
I leveled up when it ended.
I leveled up by letting go.
I leveled up when you left.
I leveled up in your absence.
I leveled up when it ended.
I leveled up by letting go.
I leveled up when you left.
I leveled up in your absence.
I leveled up when it ended.
I leveled up by letting go.
I leveled up when you left.
I leveled up in your absence.
I leveled up when it ended.
I leveled up by letting go.

SHE, BESIDE A FIRE

I thought about you as soon as I woke up. I could see the light from the morning sky pushing itself through the corner of the window, and in the silence, I heard your voice greeting me with a tone of peace and joy. I feel you with me throughout the day; your silent presence fills the room like the most beautiful fragrance. You've become the author of my every thought lately; you tell me stories without even speaking. Stories about where you are and what you're feeling. They flow out of me here for the world to see for all to witness.

I love that our connection at this moment is inspired by this genuine desire for a love that lasts. I love that our connection comes from the idea of something deep and profoundly pure.

SHE, BESIDE A FIRE

You know what? There were so many quiet moments happening in my heart, and so often, I found myself whispering your name, hoping the wind would carry my love to you.

SHE, BESIDE A FIRE

She's not ashamed of what she's been through. She wore her scars like the most beautiful attire. A stunning dress made from hellfire with a fabric made to sustain anything her enemies put in her path.

SHE, BESIDE A FIRE

I just think you need to be patient with yourself. Sometimes, the heart needs more time to truly accept what the mind has discovered.

SHE, BESIDE A FIRE

she found strength in the tears
and as she cried
she used the water
to nurture the garden
in her soul

SHE, BESIDE A FIRE

the moon whispered to her
you don't need to be whole
to shine

SHE, BESIDE A FIRE

she's brilliant
she dances to the symphony
in her head
she speaks with a rhythm
of her heart
and loves from the depths
of her soul

SHE, BESIDE A FIRE

She had always been a beautiful dreamer. The kind of woman who kept her head in the clouds... loved deeply above the stars and left behind all regret beneath the earth she walked upon. No matter how often she was let down, she refused to stay there. She was always willing and ready to fly above it all.

SHE, BESIDE A FIRE

Some will look upon your light and think of you as a star but I'll be honest, the moment you showed your light to me, I knew I was meeting the moon.

SHE, BESIDE A FIRE

I love the moon, the way it moves through the darkest corners of a night sky and I like to think that you've done the same. You have also moved through the darkness while embracing your light. A light like the moon.

SHE, BESIDE A FIRE

111
222
333
444
1206
555
666
777
888
999

SHE, BESIDE A FIRE

I want to live in your thoughts and your ideas. Your memory is a rogue wave, sweeping me up and away in the most unexpected moments of bliss.

SHE, BESIDE A FIRE

You see, sometimes the most difficult part isn't actually letting go but learning to start over without being afraid to begin again.

SHE, BESIDE A FIRE

She made peace her priority; she set boundaries against anything that distracted her from cultivating bliss. She decided to build a home for herself where negativity could not cross the threshold.

SHE, BESIDE A FIRE

She dived into an ocean of her own tears because she knew of her ability to cleanse.

SHE, BESIDE A FIRE

She found her strength to illuminate during her darkest of hours. Midnight produces the brightest stars.

SHE, BESIDE A FIRE

She was made of all the things that attempted to break her, stitched together by her own will to fight, survive, learn, and heal.

SHE, BESIDE A FIRE

It was in the silence where she found her most profound strength, in solitude where she discovered a power she never knew she had.

SHE, BESIDE A FIRE

my love, you are a universe of untold stories
waiting to be written from the fire of the sun

SHE, BESIDE A FIRE

in a way
she reminded me
of a glow stick
there were times
where she had to break
to fully activate
an ability to shine

SHE, BESIDE A FIRE

love her furiously
love her without limitations

SHE, BESIDE A FIRE

and like the moon
her heart went through phases
it took some time
for her to be whole again

SHE, BESIDE A FIRE

of course there was a bit of sadness in her past
of course there'd been a fear of the future
but she discovered herself in the present
she remained mindful and practiced gratitude
for where she was and for everything she had

SHE, BESIDE A FIRE

It's never too late to walk into the light of understanding that the person you want will never deserve you. It's never too late to walk in the opposite direction of the person who has misused your love and has chosen a line of actions that can be used as proof of this belief that you deserve better. It is never too late and I know there are moments where it feels impossible to find the proper love or that idea of a relationship that doesn't require your heart to hurt. It feels like false hope, this desire to be with someone who matches the energy you bring to a relationship but you have to understand that the longer you settle, the more you feel stuck in a place that isn't aligned with the love you dream of.

I've been there, I know that struggle. I'm still there in a way. Sitting in the middle of I deserve more but also when will more arrive? What is it that I need to do in order to reach a time in my life where love doesn't equate to pain?

SHE, BESIDE A FIRE

I think it's so easy to find yourself devoted to a relationship that falls short of what you hoped for because you have this innate belief that you are capable of loving someone enough to make them love you back. You believe that if you try just a little bit harder that this person will meet you in the middle of that effort. You believe that if you fight a little harder, this person will see the value that you bring into their life but that's not how it's supposed to work. Love doesn't cause you to compromise the best things about your life or yourself. The right relationship will not force you into a cycle of low energy and vibration.

It's easy to believe that you're asking for too much when you're looking for love in a person who doesn't necessarily value you. It's easy to believe that you're asking for the impossible when the person you cling to isn't willing to provide for your basic needs, mostly the essentials of what makes a relationship work. It's easy to think that you're asking for too much when you're leaning into a space that will never have room for the abundance of love that you need.

SHE, BESIDE A FIRE

You can't supplement your loneliness by choosing to be in a relationship with someone who makes your heart feel lonely. You can't outrun sadness by choosing to hold the hand of someone who makes your heart feel empty. I think we all do this at some point in our lives. We think, I don't want to be alone and then we choose from that place, a relationship that isn't aligned with what we truly desire and we often stay there for far too long, fooling ourselves into this idea that eventually the thing we settle for can become something delightful even when that thing is not meant to last.

SHE, BESIDE A FIRE

SHE, BESIDE A FIRE

she reminded me of the sun
no matter how dark it became
she cultivated fiery flares of strength
and always decided to rise again

SHE, BESIDE A FIRE

there is poetry in your presence
you read beautifully by just existing
I love the rhythm in your expression
I feel the verse in your heart

SHE, BESIDE A FIRE

I find myself happily lost in the thought of you. Sitting still in meditation, wandering mentally, trying to find the words to describe the meaning of your refusal to give up on what you deserve. You have seen a lot of pain in your reflection, you have felt a lot of heartbreak beneath the surface and yet here you are, reading these words. This is the moment where you realize that I'm talking to you about you. This is the moment where you remember who the fuck you are. A Goddess remembering that she can heal herself. A woman remembering that she can fly. A Queen, a warrior. A body remembering its magic. I love the way you exist. I love the way you show up in the world and I dedicate this moment to you.

SHE, BESIDE A FIRE

she knew exactly
when to be hellfire
and when to be holy water
your experience was based solely upon
the way you made her feel

SHE, BESIDE A FIRE

sometimes, the only way to learn
how to swim is to drown
the only way to your strength
is to be pushed toward
a moment of weakness
the only way to catch your breath
is to lose it for a moment

SHE, BESIDE A FIRE

True love is rare because it's supposed to be. It takes an unshakable belief, a dedication, a profound devotion. Of course, you'll get hurt searching for it, but the moment you stare into the eyes of your beloved, you realize how much the pain you experienced on that journey was completely worth it. And that's what I'm waiting for; that's the experience I believe in because I believe in you. I believe you're reading this right now. Dreaming up the same thing I'm dreaming of, and I can't wait to meet you.

SHE, BESIDE A FIRE

I am but a broken pencil, attempting to write a poem on the surface of your heart. Being led by my promise to reach you no matter what happens, no matter the obstacle or hardship. I will see these feelings through.

SHE, BESIDE A FIRE

That's the thing, my love; you don't need to be saved. You, a woman who has mastered an ability to fight and survive, are meant to be discovered and appreciated for the warrior you've become.

SHE, BESIDE A FIRE

You are the artist of your own life. Remove the paintbrush from your ex's hand.

SHE, BESIDE A FIRE

Trust the truth in how others make you feel.

SHE, BESIDE A FIRE

SHE, BESIDE A FIRE

Peace doesn't mean that chaos is nonexistent. Peace is the ability to align with self in the midst of a chaotic noise.

SHE, BESIDE A FIRE

She began to extend and strengthen her roots, a growth that deepened beneath the surface of where no one could see. This is how she mastered the ability to bloom no matter the circumstance.

SHE, BESIDE A FIRE

I know he doesn't love you. There are moments when you are distracted from experiencing the things you want to feel, and real love is not an obstruction.

SHE, BESIDE A FIRE

you can either have a love
that feels like thorns
or you can wait for a love
that is in constant bloom

SHE, BESIDE A FIRE

she was mindful
she remained present
she figured out how
to see the masterpiece
in every moment

SHE, BESIDE A FIRE

your heart knows the answer
silence your mind, be still
and follow yourself

SHE, BESIDE A FIRE

her evolution was so great
that those who wanted to diminish her light
could not recognize the Goddess
that stood before them
more powerful than anything they'd known
a brilliant light, brighter than
she'd ever been

SHE, BESIDE A FIRE

the weeds are toxic ties
that you must cut
from your garden
in order to grow

SHE, BESIDE A FIRE

I just think you're built for love. This is why no amount of heartbreak can destroy your belief in the kind of love you deserve.

SHE, BESIDE A FIRE

I want to find you when I'm lost. I want to recognize you when everything else feels unfamiliar. I want to see love's face when I stare into your eyes. My future is at your fingertips; I'd know what's to come when you touch me.

SHE, BESIDE A FIRE

They can't always see it, the language of your essence isn't easy to comprehend. For it is only meant to be experienced by someone who is willing to put in the effort to understand.

SHE, BESIDE A FIRE

You're just not for everyone and everything about you is brilliant, there is a genius in your design. And as you read this, as you grant me permission to take up space in your mind for this moment, I hope you feel seen despite how lonely it's been or how heavy your heart has felt as you try to navigate this profound sense of self.

SHE, BESIDE A FIRE

I say all of this to say that you are rare and beautiful in the most powerful way, and I hope you take this moment to embrace your light, your existence, and your magic.

SHE, BESIDE A FIRE

You thought it was a loss, but in the absence of the person who refused to care for you properly, you discovered that you could be the source of your own happiness and peace.

SHE, BESIDE A FIRE

There is a love that exists that will not cause you to question how real it is. There is a love that will not force you into confusion or delusion. A love that will match the intensity in your heart, a love that will never end once it starts.

I hope it finds you sitting still. I hope it finds you while you heal. I hope you understand that you're worth it. Perfection doesn't exist but the fit will be perfect.

I want you to click away from this post with the realization that you are genuinely deserving of being loved properly. Be patient love. It's coming.

SHE, BESIDE A FIRE

Are you happy with him? Does he make your heart race? Is he nurturing your soul enough to inspire your heart to grow? Is he consistent in the truth, has he remained transparent? And have you answered no to any of the questions you just read?

I want to see you happy even if it's not with me.

I want to see your heart thrive because after everything you've gone through, you deserve to be loved in the most beautiful of ways. You give so much, you've fought so hard. You tell your truth, you wear your scars. You love deeply as if you've never been hurt. You've tried even when your effort remained overlooked and so at the very least, you should be loved with the highest intensity and a depth so great you feel it at the core of your very being.

SHE, BESIDE A FIRE

How is it that you help me remember things that haven't happened yet? There's something in your movement that tells me my future's set. A mutual understanding, enlightenment and depth. An ease, a release... like returning to one's breath. I wander into your mind at the moments you need me most. A healing balm for the heart, the mind and soul. So if there's ever a moment where you're stuck and feel alone. I'm with you always and this is how I'll let you know. Think of you in prayer and daily meditation. Our conversations have become the highest form of elevation. And so, I offer you these words as a form of dedication. I'm sorry it took this long, I'm sorry to keep you waiting.

There's so much more I could say but I'll share throughout time. I'm fully present in this moment, so as to not miss the signs. I think you represent a peace that has escaped me for years. I say this because the last bit of noise was rendered obsolete when you appeared.

SHE, BESIDE A FIRE

The fire was growing silently beneath the floorboards and behind the walls; inside the attic, the smell of smoke, though faint, had begun to fill the air. As time went on, the fire expanded, and the heat from the flames began to bite at your skin.

And you tried to put it out, but no amount of effort mattered. You stood there in the living room, weary, witnessing the windows shatter. Heart battered and bruised. Your soul is tired, and your mind, confused. You are contemplating moving forward with a fear of everything you'll lose, but then it happens. Something clicked from within a moment of clarity. The end is where you begin.

SHE, BESIDE A FIRE

The end is where you begin.
The end is where you begin.
The end is where we begin.
The end is where you begin.
The end is where you begin.

SHE, BESIDE A FIRE

Listen to that voice; the inner workings of what you are will always deliver to you the answers to your most pressing questions.

Listen to that voice, for it truly knows what you are searching for, and it will lead you in the right direction.

It wasn't easy, but the fire, initially meant to destroy her, became a place of warmth, a torch, a light, a guide to something better. That fire, so destructive, had become a moment to forge a much stronger path. The silence became a sort of song in which she decided to dance.

SHE, BESIDE A FIRE

(she takes one last glance at the fire, and in a soft tone, she hears the words, " the end is the beginning..."

(she turns to see where the voice is coming from...)

FADE TO BLACK, THE END...

Made in the USA
Las Vegas, NV
28 March 2025